WE WORE
DRESSES

BCC
PRESS

BY COMMON CONSENT PRESS is a non-profit publisher dedicated to producing affordable, high-quality books that help define and shape the Latter-day Saint experience. BCC Press publishes books that address all aspects of Mormon life. Our mission includes finding manuscripts that will contribute to the lives of thoughtful Latter-day Saints, mentoring authors and nurturing projects to completion, and distributing important books to the Mormon audience at the lowest possible cost.

In a poem near the end of Marilyn Bushman-Carlton's *We Wore Dresses*, the speaker says, "I'm digging out, making room for extravagant abundance / of nothing at all, for the sharper relief of absence" ("The Solace of Letting Go"). There is, however, a delicate blueprint by which we arrive at this sly renunciation. The poems earlier in the collection show in unsparing terms how girlhood shapes womanly experience; they are indispensable for reading the later poems, more yielding and open. The book is a cabinet of wonders: even the poems that render the most painful moments of the soul's—and body's—progress gleam with magical naming. In "Murmuration," the speaker, witnessing starlings weaving their patterns in the sky, says, "All hail and hallelujah I say to no one / & divine what I can from these ordinarily / misbehaving birds, praise their bonanza / of magnetic plainsong". I am drawn to and enlivened by these generous, musical, sharp poems.

—Lisa Bickmore
Poet Laureate, State of Utah

Marilyn Bushman-Carlton's fourth poetry collection, *We Wore Dresses*, is the work of a mature artist completely in command of her craft. These poems explore every stage of the poet's life from girlhood to retirement and every relationship from daughter to wife to mother to grandmother with compassion, elegance, and wit. This work is not to be missed.

—Holly Welker
editor of *Baring Witness: 36 Mormon Women Talk Candidly about Love, Sex*, and *Marriage and Revising Eternity: 27 Latter-Day Saint Men Reflect on Modern Relationships*

Marilyn Bushman-Carlton offers these poems like seashells on the palm of a child at the beach for the first time, glimmering in their tender specificity. A young girl plays on the "tricky bars." A mother is touched when her young adult son wants to watch again a movie with her that she introduced him to as a child. A group of young parents learn from a Sunday School teacher who has lost an arm. A woman in an aging body contemplates whether to give up her manicures. And here, too, are many fascinating landscapes—St. George, France,

Ethiopia, an old-fashioned bathroom. The collection is a mosaic of moments—delightful, rueful, nostalgic, poignant. But the real joy is in how we get to the universal through these specifics—the tutelage of childhood, living in a body, cultural expectations and restrictions. After reading, I feel as if I've had a long sanity walk with a good friend, the kind you can empty yourself to and who helps you pick up each concern and turn it to the light.

—Darlene Young
author of *Count Me In*, *Here*, and
Homespun and Angel Feathers;
winner of the Association for Mormon Letters Award for
Outstanding Contribution to the Field of Mormon Letters

We Wore Dresses is a rich collection of poems, full of Marilyn Bushman-Carlton's wisdom. The collection demonstrates that she has lived well and loved enormously. It begins by examining what was both endearing and annoying for girls growing up in the 1960s (dresses always; physical "exercise" that kept girls weak; wanting to be thin like Audrey Hepburn, Jackie Kennedy and Twiggy; MIA girls being made responsible for boys' sexual behavior; and hoping to find something in life to be good at). But the collection goes much farther than its title subject. The poems show continual growth and exploration for Marilyn and her family, and they embody great love and insight. The true partnership Marilyn and her husband share is demonstrated in several poems, especially "Statistics Say You'll Die First." Family poems abound, and there are some I will remember for the rest of my life. The poems are also superbly wrought, with lines like "lizards and toads lead lower-case lives" and "the faintest ripple   a spilling whisper / a soap bubble   dispersing" to describe a quickening baby in her womb.

This is a collection that is meant for reading and rereading, with new rewards each time it is experienced.

—Susan Elizabeth Howe
author of *Infinite Disguises*

WE WORE DRESSES

POEMS BY

MARILYN BUSHMAN-CARLTON

For information contact
By Common Consent Press
972 East Burnham Lane
Draper, Utah 84020

Cover design: Jeremy Ames
Book design: Andrew Heiss

www.bccpress.org
ISBN-13: 978-1-961471-21-4

10 9 8 7 6 5 4 3 2 1

—for Joyce Ellen Davis (1939–2022)

—and, always, for my family

"... the girl on a swing ... longs to leave
yet she longs to return; she asks to go higher."

—Faith Shearin, "Girl on a Swing," *Telling the Bees*

The Poems

We Wore Dresses   1

One

Girls' Gym   4
Thin   7
Desire   8
Waiting   10
Dear Undiscovered Talent   12
The Family Hands   14
Susie   15
Early Love   17
The Proposal   18
Tug of War   20
It's a Girl   22
Cleave   24
One Missing   26
Quickening   27
Irresistible Burdens   28
Just a Boy   30
Passage   32

Music Comes for the Oldest Son 33
Watching "The Elephant Man" 34
My Body in Motion 36
Shopping for a Valentine while in a Fight 37
Sunday School 39
My Maiden Name 41

Two

Hair Narratives 44
In the Middle of it All, Who Thinks of Endings? 46
Guatemala 48
Sea Motifs 50
To Be a Cow in Switzerland 52
Peach Alley Court, Apartment 218 53
Horizontal 55
Not Sleeping in Addis Ababa 56
Forget-Me-Nots 58
The Beginning of Us 60
Our Spot in Millcreek Canyon 62
Barbed Wire and Cardinals 64
Learning to Touch 66
My Mother (who is in Heaven) Meets Heavenly Mother 67
My Father's Trombone 70
Judas 72
Breadbox Ghazal 74
Various Cakes 76
Her Breasts 78
The Time Has Come 79
Who Needs You Anyway? 80
A Found Poem 81
Each Cup a Story 83
Late Night Text from My Daughter 84

Three

Forecast	86
And Where Were You?	87
Cinnamon in a Pandemic	88
Winter Meet-ups with Carole during the Covid Pandemic	90
Polio	92
Marriage in Stacked Couplets	95
Mid-November Rain	96
Murmuration	97
The Basic Tune of the Sparrow	98
I Settle into My Other Years	99
The Solace of Letting Go	100
Procedure	101
The Dermatologist	103
At the Nail Salon	104
Lingering	105
The Granddaughters Wear My Clothes	107
O Morning Glory	108
Statistics Say You'll Die First	109
Home Again	112
Acknowledgements	113

We Wore Dresses

We wore them everywhere. Learned the lay of the land
in them. They reigned in our closets.
Every day to school we wore them. On the tricky bars,

stifling the urge to hang from the natural
bend of our knees.
Scenting starch and cotton, we learned division in them,

in sashes and wide hems, diagrammed sentences,
driving pencils—
our legs crossed stony tight because of them—

down the dead-end streets
where prepositional phrases and adverbs belonged.
In dresses we were careful, won few scars or bruises,

collected even fewer tales of swift licks, shattered bones.
No scrabbling to the rescue in a dress,
or scorching to home base. We played jacks

with bouquets of skirt bunched
in the V of our legs. Dresses covered
intricate bodies: puffed-sleeve dresses, dresses

with gathered skirts, pleats like Japanese fans.
We were flowers: angel trumpets, fuchsia, inverted tulips.
Lithe teenage bodies in baby dolls, twirly skirts, sheaths.

We were lavished with long, elegant versions
for balls and proms—
satin and glitter, chiffon and shine.

How exquisite we felt—our throats bared and blushed;
the way, with our fingertips, we lifted the skirts like ladies.
How disarmed we were,

our soft flesh belted,
an orchid stuck near our made-up faces, perfumed
and pinned carelessly close to our hearts.

But what of these rooms,
with their smell of feet and crush of complex dresses,
live voices inside them like pockets of snow:

—Kathy Fagan, "Widows and Brides"

Now you are tangled up in others
and everything you do
has some weird failure in it.

—Rumi, "The Guest House"

Girls' Gym

—circa 1960s

We make mothy circles
with outflung arms,
lift a leg, teeter,

rotate an ankle.
Reach, the teacher says,
and our fingers grasp air.

Imagine picking cherries.
Phantom cherries:
bite-sized, sweet.

Wilt, she says.
Let your arms dangle.
Relax into it.

We're pendulums swinging;
cowslips nodding.
Breathe deeply. In and out.

Rows of girls bend.
Pliable girls
with round yielding arms

meant to fall luringly
from sleeveless dresses,
strappy formals.

Or do we bow?
Do we bow in straight rows?
Straight and narrow rows,

following the command
to dangle?
Now we're on the floor,

our legs cooled by wood,
our fleshy thighs
held open with our hands

1,2,3,4,5 . . . ,
purple shorts snapped
around our sun-hungry

wholesomeness.
We flex toes into ourselves.
Hold. Hold. Hear almost-whispered

verbs: *flex, lean, circle, pivot.*
Mrs. Walker says *extend,* but the gym has walls.
We firm our torsos

with modified push-ups and sit-ups,
few enough to keep us
decorative/uncompetitive/

weaker than/softer.
On our backs, knees bent, we lift
pelvises toward the impossible ceiling.

Lift, hold . . . SQUEEZE . . . ,
our oven-wombs pre-heat.
Upon our ribs, below our lips,

above our hips: our breasts!
Our breasts are cushions. Saved,
bra-bound, future-husband cushions.

Baby cushions. We stand
to work the muscles behind them:
Chests forward, arms back,

push 1,2,3 . . . palms together, flat. Push and hold . . .
Our girlfriend chant: "We must
develop our busts!"

We're on our knees, an arm raised, a leg.
We're puppies. Happy puppies.
Breathe.

We exercise just long enough
to pink our cheeks.
Oh, how we blossom

in our allotted little plots!
So modestly we blossom.
Cool down. Feel yourselves melt.

Slow down, down
slowly, so
slowly we

hardly
feel our bodies
freeze.

Thin

More than boys, a pretty face, or food, I wanted to be thin
like Audrey Hepburn, with hips dangerous as blades,

like Jackie Kennedy, shoulders cutting through a crowd.
Most of all, I wanted to be thin like Twiggy

with shorn hair and translucent skin dotted with brown
freckles. I wanted taut cheeks pinched rosy, eyes round

as the pies I was reluctant to nibble. I wanted breasts
like small determined fists, dresses stylishly hung

from collars grazing them, exclamatory androgenous ties
falling between. I wanted to float light as a lifted finger

around a dance floor, to rise soundlessly as yeast. Wanted
to drape my bones in beautiful clothes. My body

had to merit each furnishing. To mollify its cravings,
I settled for a single-serve soft ice cream, a strip of taffy

slowly raised like manna to my mouth, black
licorice split into strips and consumed like a sacrament.

Wanting to freeze my body into its adolescent stupor, I gave up
things I didn't need: sauces, butter, beef, and began

to carry with me a washed apple, a substitute to savor bite
by delicious bite, its pips, piquant core, salubrious flesh.

Desire

The Mia Maid teachers pretend girls don't have it,

even though we reek of it,
even though it oils the fasteners of our necklaces,

stains the buttons of our blouses,
skids on our shoes to dances in church parking lots.

The teachers are stuck on making us stewards for the boys,
blaming our bodies for boys' out-of-control urges.

But under our calm corporeal skin, it whispers.
In lessons about love, we hear *desire,*

the portal into love, the portent of everything
we'll ever want or need; the mustard seed of bliss.

Over and over, they try to tamp it down
until we're smooshed like handled cake.

Still, it escapes from every kind of music: blues,
rock and roll, swing. Hymns. We stand all amazed

at pictures of young David's muscled arms,
Samson's flowing sun-livened hair,

Nephi's thigh-grazing pelt.
Desire rubs its misery into our skin, into

Jezebel's messy bed, into risible thoughts
of the blind leading the blind into a roadside ditch.

It's in Jordan's placid water; it lights the city on a hill.
Desire brushes our right and left cheeks,

floats in the whale's belly, pours like forty days and nights
    of rain.
It lives in our body temples like wicked golden mammon,

like precious gifts of frankincense and myrrh.

Waiting

Even winter comes slowly. Leaves amble
in the dinge of early dark.
At sixteen I'm living a glum passive death

stuck and out of place in a new town
and, tonight, in the local drugstore
working at my first real job.

Because it's Thursday a man I've learned to loathe blows
with the icy draft through the front door.
He saunters to the soda fountain,

and, as usual, orders one pineapple milkshake.
When I serve him,
I catch a scant human smell

rising from his bleached-out work shirt.
When I ask if he'd like two spoons, he declines.
As is the pattern, one of his children is with him.

A daughter, in an overlarge dress with pinked sleeves,
waits on the stool beside him
blankly staring at what's left of the day's cupcakes and donuts

under a smudged glass dome.
The man dips his silver spoon into the large
Coca Cola glass that narrows at the bottom,

lifts it lazily to his stingy lips.
The shake lolls on his tongue, then wanders
past his callous heart.

He dribbles the other half of the pale-yellow treat
from the tall metal mixing container
into the emptied glass, filling it, again, to the top.

Oh! how I want to give the girl something to eat,
or feel, some flavor of joy.
But in this enduring surround of winter,

I can't conjure a sip of anything.
She and I can only watch this man
waste her precious years

while he dips and lifts his spoon,
while he savors taste after taste after taste.

Dear Undiscovered Talent

Where within my genetic possibilities do you hide?
Why elude me when I ask, even beg,
bowl in hand,
to be your instrument?

Show me just one thing I might do.
Come in any form: perhaps a girlish figure,
slim neck, strings of course, and a bow.
Let me learn

to coax from it a gypsy jig, pent-up tears,
to know if I can stand in haloed light,
wear plaudits gracefully.
Come to me toothsome clad in lacquered black,

cumbersome as a monument, yet
flared as a Caribbean shore. Electrify the hairs
of my nape with a soprano voice, wreathe
the metropolitan halls of my dreams,

rapture me with sober floes.
Raise the Titanic up from my soul.
Dance to me on fat silver taps, pedestrian Keds,
slipper on over in pastel toe shoes,

slide on second-hand skates.
I'll do my best to float like a swan, unimpressed
with my sinuous neck, my regalia of down.
Come sotto voce

a magician, a gymnast, a knitter of yarn. Let me twirl a baton.
But don't let me walk by myself,
stand lonesome, leafless, feet mired in mud.
Show me a partner for life, that thing of myself, an identity

to describe, accompany, and burnish my name.
Gift me a passport to carry, spend as I can
on the lackluster world. Something charming,
challenging, mine. I'll do the work.

The Family Hands

are predisposed to use,
have a weakness for a job well done,

don't bother with gloves in hot dishwater,
in garden dirt, soiled toilets.

Our hands like hammering,
tightening, brushing, paring.

Lust after needles, mops
pruning shears, pitchforks, the hose.

Embrace bloody sirloin,
seasoned and put to roast, anything

they can coil around, dig into, gut, core.
Our hands want coal dust-coated house walls,

splattered dairy-barn walls;
young corn with layers of husks,

knifing out the worms in it, washing,
slicing, filling boiling pots with cobs of it.

Our hands crave duty, satisfaction,
accomplishment, crave tools

holding place in a job
to resume come morning

when they'll move smoothly on to the next
and the next and the next until we die,

finally resting across our bodies
in the narrow fulfillment of our coffins.

Susie

She appeared our senior year out of the blue
sky of the Texas panhandle
with her *y'alls,* her Karmann Ghia,
and bursting with beautiful foolishness.

Soon we had the storage behind the seat
filled with empty pop bottles,
and a damaged muffler we'd attacked on a whim.
She talked the wildest boy in school into

taking us for a ride in his car. On the narrow
lower road without shoulders,
the speedometer was on its way to Mt. Timpanogos
until he saw my fear.

One day Susie declared my hair the color to frost—
we called it frosted then because it looked
like Jack Frost's scintilla those fleeting
spring days that made us ache.

We bought the swim cap, some kind of bleach,
a crochet hook, and then I sat, my trust, if not complete,
simply idling in the vanishing year.
She plied the pieces from the punctured cap

without a care, and then the highlights came.
Then, a shocking car wreck immediately after
she'd noticed other cars had slowed on the snowy road,
we flew across like an arrow aimed for the grassy ditch

that held us like a cradle, overturned, but unhurt.
Years later, a guy she'd briefly dated told me
she'd tried to get him to run away with her to Vegas.
And then she did, with someone else. After graduation

my willful, foolish friend who gave me highlights
I'd keep forever in my hair, ran away
with a boy from a band, a boy who ran away again,
leaving her stranded with a baby.

Early Love

Look, it's you again, standing out in the crowd
of high school classmates from wherever you are,

each part of you so soon memorized
and manacled by my passible teenage heart.

There, in the Little Theater, the library,
in the crowd at Watties after school,
I'm helpless to unlatch the force of you,

to still the vibes, the inexplicableness
of what it is about you I'm resigned to always crave.

You bob up from the rest like balsam,
reach the itch, steal the scene from any guy I might yet love.

I feel it, too, you equally aware of where I am,
both of us pesky urges that cannot be amused
or yet utterly embraced.

How we strive to parse the too-young, anxious
bulging in our hearts,

the distant horizon lush with us,
though anyone can see the lank futility
to halt such trouncing passions in our hearts,

the lofty notions, the yet to discover
fulness of all love could haply be.

The Proposal

They celebrated with feverish Mormon kisses—
always wanting more, but settling
for tonguing an ear, lunching on a sweaty philtrum,
lip-gnawing the plateau of a nose—
then began to talk about the future.
One subject he raised—
who would make the big decisions when they wed—
cocked an eyebrow of the soft, sexy moon,
spawned its hasty raffish turning,
and made her scramble to finesse her words,
besotted as she was with this man she meant to marry.
She quietly turned them out: *partners, equal, fair.*
He tossed back: *priesthood and motherhood, nature, nurture,*
and the words hovered in the vast between.
Maybe his vigilance was insightful,
as was hers, pushing back
just enough to keep them who they were and had to be,
he with all the footage of his life—

his dad, his coaches, the principals, authority
in its eternal attire at church—
and she, with background clatter of her own—
her mother often wanting, the lady teachers
asking permission, the silly lessons everywhere
that taught her how to play the game,
to show her how to make him (or was it her?)
think he'd won.
He wanted to know. She punted,
tantalizing words like *partnership, negotiation, compromise*
marinating in the late 1960s February air.

Tug of War

Sleep eludes my weedy, raw, depleted body,

though it begs for it, and though our new baby
finally purrs in my arms. My husband of a year,

just back from his stint of basic training,
breathes in and out without bother.

I wonder what lies ahead for our little family
after weeks in our in-laws' house, where all day long

the baby cries with colic. I have no idea when or even if
this miserable little stranger will coo or smile,

if she'll lie in her crib awake, not crying,
and kick her fat legs with happiness.

Too often, when she finally naps
in the porta-crib placed in the living room,

my mother-in-law steals in with a fusty avocado afghan
doubled in half, and covers her, even though

her forehead mists with sweat in the August heat.
I sneak in barefoot, broach the blue crib

and lift the suffocating thing away,
exposing my baby's perfectly adequate white undershirt

and hemmed diaper with ducky pins.
This woman who isn't even my mother

straggles out of sight, posed to crush me.
The slightest whimper and my baby's gone again,

smothered in her grandmother's spongy bosom,
in cloying baby talk,

that merciless horsey dance of prance and sway,
in hands that calm her stiff, distressed torso to compliancy,

allowing both my baby and me, albeit briefly, to sleep.

It's a Girl

—for my firstborn, 1970

With the colic gone
and the three of us on our own,

your tummy muscles and fists unknot, and you give
to the roost of my lap the whole of you:

your pudgy thighs, first smiles,
your brown eyes fixed and flared, your whetted ears.

Just like that, you are my daughter, my alpenglow,
my heart, my raison d'etre, my comfort

in the sanctum of our rental house
far from everyone we know.

How beautiful you are waking up
older every day, your father's spitting image until

your legs pilot your walker,
you take first steps, and finally toddle by my side.

Still your father's spitting image until
cadences of songs and rhymes

babble from your mouth with my inflections.
Until your hands crack eggs, turn pages,

cartwheel when you talk, toss stones.
There in the middle of nowhere: a coterie of two

through diurnal verbs of patchwork pansies,
slobbering dogs, misbehaving twilight stars.

Together past tickle-toe leaves
toward the mythical eye of heaven.

My nirvana, my *pickle-ee*.
You and me and everything all day.

My hungry, precocious, muddy little warrior,
my *little woman* learning to chase all the dreams.

Cleave

—for Jacob, 1976

After the long labor and punishing birth
and shortly after the initial shock

of seeing his precious lip split,
his innocent face not fully knit together,

I'm given a shot to dry up my milk.
A brief visit from a plastic surgeon about what's to come,

and I'm sent home with a glass tube to feed my baby—
a bulb at one end, a flexible tube at the other—

and instructions to mix a little Gerber cereal
with formula to slow it down

when I place it at the back of his tongue.
Because he is our fourth, and because

my breasts are empty as a man's,
his father and I take turns with nightly feedings.

Jacob is all mine in the soft, April light
those first reluctant shifts,

the rest of the house slumbering.
He doesn't fuss while the milk warms and I change his diaper,

and then surrenders—his head to the bowl of my hand,
his floppy body to my lap—

and takes the nourishment gratefully.
When he's sated in that pose, I study him,

breathe the infant tang of him,
finger-trace his features

and bend to kiss each one, his fontanel,
his father's forehead, his rashy nose and biscuit cheeks,

his birth-squished ears,
and then his mouth, my lips lingering there.

He's had a hard time, too—the posterior birth, wide
shoulders, the extra padding from the weight I'd gained—

and doesn't know there's more hurt yet to come.
At six weeks they repair the cleft

and keep him in the hospital another two so it can start to heal.
When he comes back to us, most of spring lost—

a metal bridge taped over the incision,
his sleeves safety-pinned to his diaper—

he's fraught from crying. At first,
we are cleft. I cannot press him breast to breast—

now the closure must hold its seal—
and have to improvise,

cleaving his back to my front, his body's heat,
his beating heart against my own.

I don't know how it is on his father's nights,
but I soothe him fiercely that way,

tuck him into me. Body and soul, he folds, his arms clipped,
a hand rooting for one of my fingers to cleave to.

One Missing

My second-grade daughter waits
—for what? the world to end?
Or just the day's last bell?

She's sheltered in the girls' bathroom,
her stomach a circus of tricks.
The hair ornaments she loved

on our summer stop at the Four Corners
are now too unique.
When Mrs. Simons sees Jari's vacant desk,

she leaves the rest of the class to find her.
Then, undeterred, sends
our daughter's favorite friend to admire

the ornaments. Then two more girls,
clusters of three, five, eight . . .
Then boys who tumble out in little teams

until all twenty-four 7-year-olds with big front teeth
ring around her in the hall—sweet
whistling machines that know their work;

drum-roll hearts, each carrying its own aplomb,
each approving, as it can, the leather bangles.
They coax and coo, sing poems and paragraphs

until the floor gives beneath their eager feet.
Mrs. Simons' solid blue eyes say *Years of this*
and *What's a day* as the climbing sun

warms the patient classroom,
lights the paper mâché solar system,
the dumb books, the wooden rulers.

MARILYN BUSHMAN-CARLTON

Quickening

—the stage of fetal growth at which
life is felt by the mother

the faintest ripple   a spilling whisper
a soap bubble   dispersing

a flutter   a ruffling   a flicker

and I knew   I knew
the way I know the hour without seeing a clock's hands or
  hearing its chime

the way I know from a sound sleep
that one of your siblings stands beside my bed   and waits

a scratch from inside an egg; from inside me
a bashful tap: your announcement   your hello

your family circling the table   a lull in supper's whirlwind

just like you to wait your turn   to listen first
no matter how monumental your news

more than a hint   soft as sun warming my skin
the consciousness of a scribble   a peek

our first shared moment

the first time you chose me

Irresistible Burdens

The children would be asleep
by the time we pulled away from the jammed parking lot,

the AC blasting. In numb, exhausted slumber,
they'd congeal in lumpy masses, separated

only by the dreams that swaddled them.
Gone for another year: the tidal wave, the fun house,

the log flume, the Jet Star they'd have to earn,
with inches, the right to ride. Just a dream: the shave ice,

the cotton candy risen like magic from paper cones.
Home again, their dad and I would saddle over our shoulders

the youngest two, little boy bags of storage wheat or puppy
    food,
and lay them, still deep in sleep,

on their bed beneath a 40-watt puddle of light.
In turn, we'd pull each dead arm through its sleeve,

each limp leg through its wrinkled opening,
each wobbly head through the top of a soiled shirt.

MARILYN BUSHMAN-CARLTON

Remove each closed-toe shoe, each damp, odorous stocking.
No baths those late nights, just soaped washcloths

over salty, sun-smeared hands and faces,
under fringes of moppy forehead hair,

soap on their spongy, spent feet. Then jammies
over the irresistible burdens of their abandoned bodies,

their delicious relentless helplessness
that defined our then young lives.

Just a Boy

—my oldest son reacts to feminism

He's just a boy, my oldest son,
following two sisters. A tattered warrior,
I'm focused on making sure the girls

have chances I didn't.
My eyes are on the lookout, my vision wide,
my pique often pointed and raw.

Meanwhile, my confused boy
draws rudimentary maps
of the neighborhood, his world for now,

and is trying to find his way through it.
I know it's not always easy for him,
and maybe he thinks I don't see that, so far,

his boy body has brought a windfall of nothing
to his buttered lap, his clement days.
The house we live in chants with books, signs:

Well-behaved Women Seldom Make History,
A Woman's Place is in the House . . . and in the Senate
weighting the place where he dreams.

He sees me take his sisters
to marches, candlelight vigils, leaving him
an airy subtraction

with hints of blame for being who he is.
My son who often pauses in the middle of his play
to pluck a flower to bring to me.

My son, the blue burn of his eyes
exposing the depth of his peeled-plum heart,
its minor notes,

the surrounding sclera white
as his personality: *peacemaker, honest, cautious,*
one who hesitates to claim his share.

Passage

Cold mornings he leaves
without a coat, not even a sweater
over his light cotton shirt,
his exposed arms savoring
the bite of protest,
the fight against surrender.
Shoulders hunched, he
muscles through the cold,
his hands tunneled
into his pants pockets,
the tempo of his steps rising
as he rounds the corner
to junior high.
His head leads, bare
but for the fierce doggedness
pulling him on with something
like pleasure,
his blue eyes wild
as the sky's bitter beauty.

Music Comes for the Oldest Son

Chris comes to the youth symphony
lugging his polished shoes, his pockets bulging
with woe. Wears a halo of bees.

Passing the do-not-touch Chihuly glass, the gold leaf,
his feet thud the carpet like clubs.
His glum adolescent face hosts eyes

dark enough to tar the perfection
of patrons in fancy gowns, bowties.
He's come bankrupting his mother's best efforts

to indulge her vanity, her chance to shine—
the five children gussied to flawlessness.
While his siblings yield to the razzmatazz and pomp,

this one flumps into his plush seat
where he duels with the knives of his ironed collar,
scuffles with the buckle of his belt.

But the music finds him in the shadows,
swoons its balm around the whole of him,
accepts his despair like someone who loves him.

It comes bursting in an outdoor voice he knows,
comes banging, whooshing, outraged, flashing, dancing dizzily,
skittering, trickling, weeping, dreaming,

comes talking smack with his mudpuddle and potato bug heart,
his ten-year-old sunbaked soul. Comes befriending,
comes listening.

Comes bringing a new map
beyond the boundaries of his neighborhood world,
comes to accompany him through life.

Watching "The Elephant Man"

We'd wanted them to feel discomfort,
to learn their empathy,

wanted them to pull another's pain
through their smooth young bodies,

let it nestle there
beside their brilliant possibilities.

Here was a human, John Merrick—
he had a name—hidden within

a hideous cauliflower-like covering.
The movie was black and white, perfect

we thought, they'll get the message:
a good man, a sympathetic doctor

to befriend him, and a crowd of
common individuals who go along with mischief.

Justin, our youngest, shy of seven,
gulped the horrors in

as he watched this man, this soul
with the sad tuft of hair,

buttonhole eyes, nice suit (tailored by a friend)
to cover the hump,

the huge distortion that prohibited him
from lying down even to sleep.

His father and I could only watch
the crowd ambush the elephant man,

MARILYN BUSHMAN-CARLTON

as a parade of voices guffawed and struck like metal lids,
as they opened the funnel of his mouth

and poured liquor in,
as women gagged to kiss his warty skin.

∼

Years later, when night settles down
over the two of us who are in the house alone,

this son, sporting new unruly whiskers,
asks if I will watch the movie with him,

again, after all this time.
What has made the memory of that movie surface now?

What's been tossed about, what nests
inside a pocket of his heart,

that confusing closed-fist muscle
Li Po says can hold everything?

He doesn't say, and I don't ask, just like I haven't asked
questions that haven't surfaced yet.

I say yes, and gratefully. It isn't often now
that he comes to me,

but it's natural when he does.
We sit apart in intimacy. No need to speak.

My Body in Motion

The postures and moves of the exercises
are new to me, and I want to see myself,

the self I hardly know these days,
the wife and mother, minder of home.

I make my way to the mirrors, front and sides,
floor to ceiling in the room, and see

my post five-quick-babies body
in motion. I watch a woman who looks like me,

but removed, the sweat
wet on her rosy face and sweat

darkening the cloth between breasts
I see for the first longtime through my own eyes.

I lean into this body held dear by a leotard
the color, I think, of tender lemons,

lean into it like I'd lean into a lover,
my face flushed and lusty,

my thighs and calves tooled for this.
Hello dancer I have never been,

hello such salty lips I've never had. Talk, loose tongue,
teach me things I've never known.

Shopping for a Valentine while in a Fight

> "It is a brave and stupid thing,
> a beautiful thing, to waste
> one's life for love."
>
> —Andrew Sean Greer,
> *The Confessions of Max Tivoli*

Stupid and waste, yes, Mr. Greer,
and possibly brave,
but beautiful, not so much,

at least today
as I search for a valentine
for the man I left behind

a slammed door on my way out
for errands and fresh air.
Among the reds and pinks,

the glitter and velvet,
the laminated, layered, and pop-ups,
the lovey-dovey, suggestive,

and singsong sentiments,
I search for understated, equivocal
words. "A heart that understands,"

"You treat me like I want to be treated,"
"You make me laugh,
feel safe, and beautiful."

These will not do,
nor will, "You take my side,"
"You soothe my worries,"

and/or especially
"You put me in a good mood."
Humor falls flat as a sexist joke,

and the promise of red wine, chocolates,
and dimmed lights . . . No way.
But when I read on a minimalistic

lightly tinted pink card,
"Through disappointments and failures,"
I think I might be getting warm.

Sunday School

Each week the teacher gave us
something to be grateful for,
for we saw,
with perfect pity,
even smugness,
certainly relief,
the conspicuous thing about him,
his missing right arm—
the urgent implication of a lesson.
We saw the cross he had to bear,
the visual aid of it,
the shrunken, shriveled stump
we imagined,
a weight inside his pinned-up sleeve.
The loss was punctuated
by his whole and useful left arm,
its hand deftly,
proudly even,
holding papers or hanging loosely
from his shoulder.
One Sunday he used the phantom arm
as a metaphor, telling how,
as a foolish teen, he'd lost it waterskiing,
how he'd cast aside the rules
allowing the rope
to twist itself around his upper arm
like a string tied taut

around a baby tooth to rip it
permanently away.
After his story—
he must have wanted this—
we rose above our ferocious pity,
rose, if just a little, into empathy.
But as resolve so often goes,
some of us began to envy
his rise along the learning curve
and the distraction
his missing arm offered.
We were young,
and anxious,
our crosses yet unknown.

My Maiden Name

Love and romance (and tradition) meant giving it up
for the privilege of belonging to someone. What girl

dressed for her wedding smells death in the white orchid,
sees imperfections in the bright diamond?

How easily I let it go, boxed it with a school play script,
pep club outfit, rogue dreams of college,

and baltered willingly into his life,
freshets babbling in streams that June wedding day.

Mrs. Somebody Else, I wrote. All those curlicues, closed
cursive loop de loops, hollow centers, but open ends, too,

I thought, to keep intact the essential girl I was,
one with history, genetic traits, one who'd won

spelling bees and school offices, whose independence
had been so fiercely collared. I became wife:

of university student, of lawyer; put my hand through
his cocked arm and walked into his dreams, his schedule,

his job that would set the boundaries of our lives. I wore
    his name
like a label sewn into his national guard clothes,

clothes I washed and ironed while he evolved in light.
His name rode correspondence through the mail, stained

our entry in the phone book, festered in the glove
    compartment.
Who could find me now? Who would need to?

There are years that ask questions
and years that answer.

—Zora Neale Hurston, *Their Eyes were Watching God*

Hair Narratives

In the elevator we share, the young French father
reaches into his daughter's hair

to untangle her clasp. His hands lift
her weeping, chaste, childhood locks

as he roots for the problem. Carefully, deftly,
incrementally, he unknots the clasp

and the hair falls into a sonata of filaments,
too many shades to decipher.

Even the dim light in the elevator
catches the sheen of her hair, illuminates his hands

as he gathers and tames it back
into the blue O-shaped ornament.

A few wispy strands stray, vibratoing,
and I think of my son and his lament

when his Elly was this daughter's size:
how he wished for a class for fathers

to learn to fix their little girls' hair.
I've seen his hands delicately lift his instrument,

seen them tighten the horsehair of the bow,
seen him arc and lace his fingers

so the strings can sing, stir and swirl
lighter than the air into which they tremble,

then disappear. I've seen blond hairs
escape the clasp ends of tip and frog

at the peak of a performance,
seen his body lean and bend, stretch and dip,

seen him wait for an opportune moment
to rest his chin on the thin wood of his violin

and quickly grasp the stray strands,
put them tidily away.

In the Middle of it All, Who Thinks of Endings?

Just this would be enough, a June morning,
clouds meandering over flat irregular roofs,

sun scintillating the once-cream walls
lining the narrow passages we thread between,

this meander—already a habit—
from our week's lodging into the flow and go, into

another day in Provence,
a pointillist's portrait of perfect leisure,

everything burnished into clarity by our short stay here:
a broom idling against a wall, a green door

rotted at the bottom (we remember to take a picture),
shutters closed against the gathering heat, a pail,

and a woman wearing what looks like my mother's
    housedress.
We're going to *Le Cheval a Bascule* where we'll wiffle and
    dither,

feet hotching as our tongues screw out the words,
la pain de chocolat, la strudel aux pommes,

most often *la croissant—plein, fromage, amandes, apfel,*
we'll try them all— our two grandchildren winking

MARILYN BUSHMAN-CARLTON

when we forget the necessary "*Bonjour!*" before we order.
Always baguettes poking from tall bags for later.

Although Eyragues seems quaint, it's merely our mindset
when unshackled from home, the atmosphere torched

with a cocktail of violet, thistle, flax, spicy mustard,
that smoky aromatic green, and strangers who pleasantly
    tolerate us.

Mostly it's the surrender of time and how we'll return
less desolate and tidy, not as dutiful or dumb,

but aching, too, with loneliness and the call to wander
back again from the boulangerie,

luxuriating in the first warm bite,
fat bronze flakes sticking to the bibs of our shirts.

Guatemala

Our driver can't get us through the city fast enough,
dodging potholes, smoky-breathed vehicles,
past odors of urine, garbage, sweat,

past broken, depleted men. The Guatemala City we'd seen
before
is bleached out now. Even boys seem old.
We won't remember grass, lampposts, birds, women, or
children.

We flee the violence tucked in the corners of our news,
flee as if being chased by drug lords, rapists, husbands,
boyfriends.
When we reach Antiqua, clean cream, blue, and coral

structures, Coca Cola signs, gustatory coffee, chocolate,
hibiscus, and limes welcome us. A man leans against his shop
smoking. Pink-brown babies feed at mothers' breasts.

In the square, a woman with heavy black hair, weaves
for a small fee, pink and white ribbons into little girls' hair.
Another coils the gray hair sweeping her feet

with perhaps thirty yards of broad grosgrain ribbon,
winds it round and round in a minute and forty-six seconds.
It rests wide and flat as a basket of trinkets mothers with
children

in tow sell from the plateaus of their heads. From our hotel
with its broad wet flowers and banana leaves, we walk to
the market
spread with palettes of corn, onions, T-shirts, and shoes.

Our driver takes us to the shore of Lake Atitlan
where we're ferried across crisp waters to the women's co-op.
We buy paintings with birds-eye views of colorful goods,

cosmetics made from herbs grown on-site,
bed coverings and bags whose cotton their hands have dyed
and spun into threads.

For the first time, Augie meets his birth family. They've
    traveled
from their lives in the mountains, an hour's journey—
walking combined with half a dozen train and bus transfers.

They wear T-shirts with English idioms.
The men's hands are deeply stained from cutting mangoes
with machetes; made old from handling sugarcane.

A baby sucks intermittently from its mother's breasts
hanging from her opened blouse, as she feasts
on McDonald's burgers and fries. Our twelve-year-old
    grandchild,

who they can't stop kissing, is the spitting imagine, they say,
of his birth mother the last time they saw her. Their daughter,
one of thousands of young women wanting a better life

lost now to the violence of the capital city.

Sea Motifs

In my son and daughter-in-law's
rental in Delaware, random
bathroom tiles have sea motifs:

a red crab, a starfish,
a turquoise seahorse,
and the usual fluted shell,

each repeated randomly
as matters of fact.
They do not insist

on any particular style,
and are not unusual or pretty,
but set a mood

that has nothing to do
with sand or reflective blue oceans.
They remind me

of a lost freedom:
they go with any color
of paint or linoleum,

and hang amicably with
three sizes of ceramic fish
and a few hard bubbles

above the tub
with its non-skid cornflowers
stuck on the bottom,

with unmatched towels
and the cedar box
I chose on a trip to Yellowstone

one long ago summer
and used for holding bobby pins.
The tiles remind me

of the house on 5th West
where I grew up,
of a time of tolerance

and cordiality
toward whatever we had
and some things we loved.

To Be a Cow in Switzerland

To be content being still,
to enjoy simply being

knee-high in pastures of salad,
dressings of dandelions, clover;
au naturel tunes—waters

romping, rumbling, gracefully stumbling
cold over slippery stones,

doing nothing
but eating my fill, pausing
to watch shirtless farmers at work.

Or to lie, slightly amused—
a dollop of blond in the sun—

at rest from routines of making
cream from campion,
cheese from the daisy,

butter of primrose and Golden Hawkes-beard.
To escape a surfeit of sun,

sudden thunder, and splurges of rain,
have my pick of sheltering trees
and a room of my own in the back of the family house.

Peach Alley Court, Apartment 218

> "Where did that dog that used to live here go?
> I thought about him once again tonight
> before I went to bed."
>
> —Shimaki Akahiko

Attempting to sleep on the sofa bed
in Alisa's apartment (once a shoe factory),
what I hear is not turn-of-the-century
shades in blue shirt sleeves
hammering leather into partnered shoes
or belts buffing steel-toed boots,

not a large loop of keys
dinging the foreman's thigh.
It isn't traffic three stories below
petering between Poplar and Market.
The town is turned down now
behind thick imperfect glass.

The windows' mammoth span
lend ambience, justify the rent,
provide deep wooden sills
from which her fern and wicker pot
of exotic herbs salute the morning sun.
What crams my sleepless head

are not past voices harmonizing
through capacious space,
now cubbied and well-insulated
with original beams and columns
stripped of paint for charm.
No, what I hear

are just the clothes dryer
finishing a midnight cycle, automatic
ice production in the fridge,
and an off-beat cuckoo counting time.
It's her sleep machine
set to the rain-forest dial,
her nightstand fan shuffling air.

It's the dainty primitive ruckus
of parakeets shifting
from perch to perch,
from one four-toed foot
to the other.

Horizontal

—Kayenta

By law, even the new condominiums must blend into this
   southern Utah
landscape, homes be earth-toned, one floor, stretching. For
   a celestial view,
hike the craggy terracotta sentinel mountains. In the valley,
   lose yourself
in the tranquil, eye-reaching lacuna. For an arching view,
   bend backward,
chin up. The shrubs are stubby, though some fool the eye
   with sun-thrust
spikes and transient knock-out blooms. Merely bushes,
   scrub, they know
their modest rank. If not, they're whittled down to size.
   Tortoises bear
their houses low, lizards and toads live lower-case lives, as
   do snakes, warning
our eyes down. In short winters the greater sparseness and
   thundering sun
call you to sit, or lie, under the mantle of bold lucid blue.
   My Swiss ancestors,
sent by Brigham Young to settle this touch-of-death
   landscape, stemmed short
and stout; to this day, stay that way, snipped and molded as
   they were by
their forebears' arduous journeys here. And their own
   pigheaded obedience.

Not Sleeping in Addis Ababa

—in Ethiopia to bring our adopted granddaughter "home"

I peer into mysterious vast black
from the barbed and gated guest house,
night broken only by scattered lights—
thousands of small islands placed
on a globe, a globe spinning like the dark women
always mopping the stairs. Their shoes

dance. Dirtying the stairs are other shoes.
My husband and daughter, their expressions black
with jet lag, don't hear the man and woman
arguing, their voices threatening the house's
quiet. There are other guests in this place—
highly recommended for families to light

between visits to the orphanage in daylight.
We'll pass the women working mops at their shoes,
and Tesfaye will drive us to the busy place
where our toddler plays and shuts her black
eyes to sleep. It's pleasant, the charitable house
where she lives, well cared for by men and women

of grace. Lunch, prepared by the women,
is served at once to the children who light
on the floor, like everything else in the house
often washed, including the step for our shoes.
Beyond high walls are dozens of black
eyes. Will she remember this place?

MARILYN BUSHMAN-CARLTON

The older children have school someplace,
and leave in tidy odds and ends. The women
and men load them into cars when the night's black
recedes; they open the gate to the light.
In the yard, other helpers with dusty shoes
fix the toddlers' hair. The house,

tight with designated cribs, is her house
for now. When we finally claim her from this place
where children look like her, and we lace her shoes
—she's been prepared a bit by the men and women—
will she be surprised at the new light?
At bright corrugated shops against the black

rain on the house falling fast, black
children like her dusting shoes, women
with sticks in place on their backs, sieving light?

Forget-Me-Nots

A dozen weeks before,
brave as a baby lion,
Laura Claire
Biftu (meaning "sunrise")
barely two, and settled
in her new mama's lap
in the back seat of a local guide's car,
rode away from the orphanage
in Addis Ababa
through tall iron gates
into dusty crowded streets.

Now, stirred into the creamy soup
of Mountain West America
in a bustling eatery,
her dark shoulders glistening
like glazed donuts
from her Gap Kids' sundress,
she breaks away from her mama,
her feet swift
and quiet as gazelle's,
and comes to a stop
at a glass partition.
Her liquid eyes fasten
to those of a girl like her
on the other side.

As if orchestrated by a tapped baton,
the two, their tight ebony curls
gathered in bundles
of forget-me-nots
and bound with rainbow bands,
lift their hands
in a slow-motion double high-five. Softly
they touch,
melting the partition
into a magic looking glass.

The Beginning of Us

—for Jari, 1994

After a year of marriage, he wants a divorce,
this shiftless son-in-law

with the thin veneer of charm.
There, I've said it, but not to my daughter. Not yet.

So far, she's defended her high school sweetheart
and is focused on what it all means

to dissolve a troth meant to be forever.
She doesn't know a single peer who's been here.

She's twenty-two.
Nothing makes sense.

Now she's asked me to meet her after work
and we sit in her car. Her words come, not bursting,

but as a slow unburdening,
measured utterances like haikus:

disconnected phone
a six-hundred-dollar bill
secret girls talk sex

And she shares now:

in the second month
key she'd found to his briefcase
pornography stash

MARILYN BUSHMAN-CARLTON

He was her best friend,
and she hasn't needed me for years.

But here she is wanting
anything I can give her.

She doesn't cry easily—oh, that we both could;
that I could take her pain in my arms, sing it away.

She was born happy, an iridescent human—
this daughter set between siblings—

and has always known just what to do,
the way, from out of nowhere

her little hands would reach to help.
I am here now holding for her

the vision of a hereafter she can't yet imagine,
holding for her this unexpected grace.

Our Spot in Millcreek Canyon

You'll see the bridge
spanning the giddy creek.
Our picnic table
has the hill behind it.

Inhale the balsam and spruce,
sulfur and newspaper,
composted leaves and cones,
the residue of fleeing chipmunks,
damp worms in the loam.

Plod up the hill's sloughed face,
steadying each step
on a half-buried rock
or hold of weeds.

Climb as high as you dare,
then use the seat of your pants
as your boat,
and your arms to oar
through the labyrinth of pines
and cousins of all sizes.

Once inside your bubble
of boiling dust, sail down,
your bottom bumping,
a wake of dust trailing.
Your feet are brakes.

Dirt powders your hair,
lodges in the philtrum
between your nose and upper lip,
blackens the oval pouch
of your mouth.

You are wilderness,
weathered fence posts,
pepper shakers,
grizzly bears.

You are tinfoil dinners
blackened by a bath
of white-hot coals.

Barbed Wire and Cardinals

"You can't lead me down that road."
—Taylor Swift

Until now, there were endings,
always happy, or at least satisfying, ones:
the cruel were punished,
white knights rushed in,
the police came,
someone was resuscitated.

Since discovering Stella and the Ku Klux Klan,
Louie Zamperini,
Ralph, Piggy, and Jack on a savage island,
and that the name of your elementary school
recognizes a Nazi camp survivor,

your sun has tumbled from heaven,
lost its halo in the fall,
and turned from gold to blood.
Your narrow shoulders balance a hammered mass.
Thieves have stolen petals from the daisies
and you can't think how to put them back.

But stars, Amelia, can't shine without darkness.
There will always be barbed wire,
but also picket fences.
There are sewers and rats, yes,
but cardinals come on the bleakest winter days.
Intensely red, they
hang their beauty out on spongy-white branches.

During the sunny days of late winter,
they trill uncomplicated lyrics:
cheer, cheer, cheer, they say,
and the world turns small again,
and becomes possible.

Learning to Touch

I was relieved when my daughter arrived at the dying,
when she got to work
saturating a hospital sponge
and pressed it inside her grandmother's cheek,
allowing her to drink. Relieved

when she moved to the bottom of the bed,
lifted the sheet and, one at a time, her feet,
bloated now and death-white,
and with lotion and unambiguous care
hydrated the dying flesh.

When in medical school, Alisa told me
how she and the other students had to learn to touch.
They practiced on one another,
and then on practice patients,

touching an arm, a leg. Gradually,
they touched the stomach, the chest,
easing their way to the consecrated place
where they would deliver babies. They practiced

until they could touch without revulsion or shame,
until it was as natural to spread the petal folds
as it was to deliver the new life
to the mother to put to her breast.

My Mother (who is in Heaven)
Meets Heavenly Mother

I picture my mother (of seven) patiently standing
in a meandering, sluggish line
(women in one; men in another)
wondering in whispers
what happens next,
their gendered bodies wearing the earth's salt.

I picture (all of them) shifting their feet
in the surround of eager blue
circled by bulbous clouds, a foaming moon,
blue and white the only absolutes.

Both lines finally thin
to zigzag through what look like Styrofoam church pews,
their inexact shapes (also) floating weightlessly.

Suddenly (but slowly, reverently) the women and the men
see advancing light
and know to bow and remove their soft-soled shoes.

I see my mother meet (for the first time)
her (our) Heavenly Mother
as the women's line tapers to the left
where She stands robed in flowing white,
her face holy and wise.

I see Her touch my mother's hand and lead her
toward a road widening to completion.

I see a multitude
of lone and dreary artifacts and trappings
tumbling through the atmosphere:

mix ing bowl and
           dinner plate frag   ments

               melting metal forks
        and pans

irons and vacuum cleaners.

                         I see scraps
          jul ien   nes

       dices   peelings

                  floor and toilet rags

threads
       brushes

         recipe and diaper shreds

                f e a t h e r s

       bottle caps. . .

I see the men, too (open-mouthed)
        their own burdens giving way—

                the strangling ties

                    the broken hammers, crooked nails

            scarred briefcases

                crumpled documents

their confident pulpits
now   s p l i n t e r e d   w o o d . . .

I see our Mother's sweeping arm
wipe away their lusterless dust, leaving just
the blue and white (the only absolutes).

My Father's Trombone

Just months after Mother died, he stood at my front door,
his trombone clutched in both hands.

He looked smaller alone, ill at ease.
It was my birthday and he was giving it to me,

if I wanted it, he said. He must have thought
I was his child who would prize it most.

I'd asked about it over the years,
trying more than once to immortalize it in a poem;

to capture what I remembered
of those long-ago Sunday afternoons

when he no longer played it in church.
It lay, a quiescent memory, on a closet shelf.

I remembered interludes of sabbath calm
before the farm and children grew and church callings

snatched even those few hours between meetings.
In my living room that day,

he opened the case the way he'd opened it
those years we children were young.

The latches still clicked distinctly.
It lay in velvet, itself tarnished as it is now

on my shelf below a favorite painting
of chrysanthemums caught by the artist in their prime.

He mentioned the inscription: *King Silver Tone,*
made by H.N. White Co. Cleveland. O—the lone O, looking

exotically old—engraved on six descending lines
on an elegantly embossed olive-oil field above the bell.

He didn't lift it from its case that day, the way he had
when we children sat at his feet around a kitchen chair

and watched with wonder as he lifted from their indented
purple beds each of its three parts:

the bell section, the slide, the chunky mouthpiece.
Nor did he assemble it with a flair of showmanship.

He didn't hold it in his hands the way he did then
nor display its forty-five inches of assembled length,

and no doubt thought I was too old now to be awed
by its full sixty-five inches if stretched along the buttery slide

to the seventh position. I wish I'd asked for that
and more: one hand on the slide brace, two fingers of the other

straddling the mouthpiece, his lips parted and pressed
  against it,
a rush of blood enlivening his face.

Judas

> "Everybody, well or ill . . . imagines a boundary of
> suffering . . . beyond which, she or he is certain life will
> no longer be worth living. [A]t various times, I could not
> possibly do without long walks on the beach or rambles
> through the woods; use a cane, a brace, a wheelchair;
> stop teaching; give up driving; let someone else put on
> and take off my underwear. [But o]ne at a time, with the
> encouragement of others, I have taken each of these . . .
> steps. . . . When I reach the wall, I think I'll know."
>
> —Nancy Mairs, *Waist High in the World*

Surviving my mother by twelve years, my father
became my perfect friend,
having evolved from the anxious and overly protective
father I'd known as a teenager.

I stopped by regularly, alone, both going and coming,
during monthly drives to southern Utah
where I escaped for quiet to write.
I developed a need to sit beside him.

Mostly, he listened
as I handed him my heart, giving it wholly to him.
He handled it carefully like a secret.
He could see inside the singular heart of his second child,
the one most like him—headstrong, quietly confident—
even as I poured out questions, even disagreements,
about the faith that was his life
and second nature.

MARILYN BUSHMAN-CARLTON

Occasionally, about a certain grievance, he asked why
I felt the way I did and listened to my explanation,
nodding, yes, he could see that.
He stayed deliberately on my side.

His mind was sound, his body agile, his heart
not only good, but strong. Then at 97
he swallowed Tums until they found the cancer.

Some of my siblings and I were with him
when the specialist told him what to expect, giving him
a few to several months.
He sat quietly
while everyone cheered him on—
he'd be reunited with his wife, our mother. His parents.

He lived alone, stubbornly took care of himself,
sometimes saying he was not ready yet. Life
was still enjoyable.

Very near the end as the two of us sat close—
his vision and hearing nearly gone—
and the distance between us was a whisper,
he confessed he wished he'd been given a choice
for treatment. That day in the specialist's office.

I felt like Judas.

Breadbox Ghazal

To guess contenders' line of work, panelists
on *What's My Line* asked, "Is it bigger than a breadbox?"

My children don't use rabbit ears, clotheslines, root cellars,
ice cube trays, iodine, diaries with keys, a breadbox.

The grandchildren eat store-bought bread from plastic bags
and have no idea what's inside my 1950's breadbox.

For size comparisons, people nowadays think:
smart phone, carry-on luggage, snowboard. Never breadbox.

To the grandchildren, mine is just a grandma thing
with cheesy kitchen motifs, not a box for bread.

When I open its red metal lid, its scent escapes,
a lost scent like mimeograph, parsnips, the breadbox.

Its small vents kept enough loaves without preservatives
fresh for days for our large family, the breadbox.

It stored plenty. Daily, we consumed the staff of life.
Necessarily prominent on the counter, the breadbox.

When it was just my parents, they bought a newer version:
wooden with a roll-top like a desk, not a cheerful breadbox.

MARILYN BUSHMAN-CARLTON

Mother died first, then Father. In the pantry we found
beside rice and Ziplocs, the nostalgic breadbox.

Hidden behind a hand mixer, paper plates, salt,
and chosen by my mother: the red-lidded breadbox.

Inside its vault: expired warranties, cancelled checks,
a Crisco can, with coils of tinfoil in the bottom of the
　　breadbox.

Inside the foil, a wad of cash the size of Father's fists.
How best to describe bounty—is it bigger than a breadbox?

Various Cakes

—Wayne Thiebaud, 1981

In a break from depicting the more sophisticated pie
and other confections favored by the lofty,
Thiebaud turned his talents from that
thinner, sliced dessert to various plump cakes—
little hummocks, mouth-watering pastimes,
some solid enough to use as doorstops.

Left behind: svelte goblets of ice cream confections,
men's ties, wobbly sunglasses.

His cakes are ritualistic offerings
painted, like women, as desirable, stylized objects,
voluptuous
bakery cakes one would hesitate to slide a knife into,
so virginal a halo might hover above them,

yet so pleasing to the eye
a *vivandiere* might uproot one from the striped blue cloth
and present it to you.

MARILYN BUSHMAN-CARLTON

Perhaps you desire
the chocolate with the cherry,
one of the buddha-like bundt cakes,
the one with icing scalloping the top,
or the one barely seen
with icing peeking from its layers,
reminiscent of women scarcely clothed,
what interests you
tantalizingly withheld
by filmy cloth, her hands,
or barely adequate doodads—

that which stirs beneath the outer layer,
the composition hidden in the depths of the cake.

Her Breasts

—a pantoum

On a bed of ribs, round and ruby-tipped they spring.
Twin appendages, they sally forth in innocence,
complex systems of glands and ducts, how uninspiring!
Front and center, oft mistaken as a gift by men.

Twin appendages, they sally forth in innocence.
Oh, riotous, frolicking flesh; bewitching potions
front and center, oft mistaken as a gift by men,
marked for nourishment; soporific cushions.

Oh! riotous, frolicking flesh; bewitching potions.
Earliest Christian emblems of sacred motherhood
marked for nourishment; soporific cushions.
Best to still them, keep their province understood.

Earliest Christian emblems of sacred motherhood.
Bras to sunder quiet fractious shifting;
best to still them, keep their province understood.
On a bed of ribs, round and ruby-tipped they spring.

The Time Has Come

Our faith is the flame on our tongues;
nourishment in the circulating air inside her van
as we drive across the country
for the fourteenth summer she's been away.

Our faith is the warp and woof
of the Scottish plaid, the threads of the English crest,
the Swiss cross of our ancestors who fled Nauvoo,
their testimonies alive in journals.

We talk of ours—hers, stacks of notebooks, Franklins;
mine, hardbacks from *Deseret Book* filled with family dailiness;
secrets, too, confided to me by her and her siblings.
"Burn them," she says.

Our faith is in her children's plans,
in what she means that her dad is a good one,
in our talk of gender, in what we eat, won't drink,
in the clothes we limit our bodies to.

This time we push further in, talk of the stuck smiles
and time-hardened pews of our faith,
the tsk-tsking, hymnbooks in pairs,
the shushed voice of our Heavenly Mother.

We talk about rashes from the heavy family plaid
and how it's lately overstretched, the patterns worn
with use, their styles and purpose lost.
We talk about the fixed architecture

and that homey smell in chapels everywhere we go,
of folding chairs in overflowing cultural halls,
ward parties, of being prepared. We talk
about the simple prayers to get us safely home.

Who Needs You Anyway?

—to my truant muse

I got by before I found
your tidy forms, apropos metaphors,
and *mots juste*.

Sure, you were the best—
read me like a sensor,
satisfied like pumpkin in Fall.

I can go elsewhere for sympathy.
There are other ways to ferret out my feelings.
I can still pay respect to little things.

It's not like giving up one of the children.

Go! Take everything that reeks of you—
the newspaper with its quips
and structured columns,

the wadded trials of paper in the trash,
the idea mosaics scattered on the desk.

Take your white spaces,
your dictionary and thesaurus.

I hate it when you sit in a corner and pout.

A Found Poem

The girl
spotted the pretty pile
of colored sand

on the floor
of the vast hall
and couldn't resist.

Never mind
it was the creation
of eight Tibetan monks

who had spent days
cross-legged on the floor
of Union Station

pouring the sand
into an intricate expression
of their faith.

They were more
than half-way done
with the *mandala*

when they ended
their work for the day
and left.

The girl
showed up
sometime later.

She did
a little tap dance
on it.

—from the *Deseret News*,
KANSAS CITY, MO, (AP)
Friday, May 25, 2007

MARILYN BUSHMAN-CARLTON

Each Cup a Story

Joe comes to mind as I stand at the kitchen sink
tearing iceberg lettuce, cold water running,

the garden a snapshot through the window.
Long ago he taught me the Italian way to crisp lettuce—

dry it twice in clean dish cloths; bundle in a third,
tuck under, chill overnight.

An embroidered handkerchief brings Grandma's babies back,
hankies finger-pressed and rolled to rock-a-bye in church.

I think of Nancy when a light trench coat
lolls over one arm like a question about the weather,

recall Mother's happiness when I open daylight's blinds,
roll pie crust sheer as stockings, scour the sink.

How many mornings do I stumble from sleep
wondering what I'll learn from someone today,

what shapeless question will be answered,
what wisdom or wonder will come to light?

Brooke blowing the hair-wrapped brush both ways
to cover the cowlick on my crown,

or the green-eyed brunette in the hot drink aisle
singing the praises of glazed lemon loaf herbal tea—

each cup a story, the box promises, *unfolding with every sip*.
Rosemary. How her warm hand wrapped my arm

when I approached her mid-conversation
with somebody else. The way she subtly held me there

like the young mothers we were held a toddler's arm
to keep him in the photo shoot.

Late Night Text from My Daughter

I'm in bed with a book,
my hair in the claws of a purple clip,
jaw beginning to slack,
the rain app pouring,
when I hear the beep.

I feel like I should get
something for Joe. What would
be appropriate? Flowers?

Her asking is a love poem,
this one with flowers.
Flowers for Joe because his father has died,

and flowers for me
to cushion and warm my sleep.
Seersucker pajama flowers
to dry and tuck away

with the orchid from her first prom,
the tattered flower jeans,
the desperate mini skirt flowers,
the Sunday best ones,

and those from the
long-shirt, cover-me-up phase,
the hair-in-her-eyes years
when she didn't ask me anything.

MARILYN BUSHMAN-CARLTON

The present becomes the past
through increments too small to measure;
suddenly something that is becomes something that was,
and the way we live is no longer the way we lived.

—Rebecca Solnit, *Recollections of my Nonexistence*

The truth is it is gone now
. . . so what details you can bring back
might have a kind of life.

—Susan Stewart, "The Forest"

Forecast

Thursday, with its *brilliant sunshine* is here,
singularly optimistic among the week's forecast:
days simply *sunny, partial, full,*
with breezes, scattered or *fluffy clouds,*
or *no clouds in sight.*

The first thing I notice
is that *brilliance* isn't silence.
It isn't cymbals either.
It's polished, creamy as a high-end sheet,
and as the hours pass, whiffs of cucumber, remaindered leaves,
liberated skin.

Brilliance isn't selfish. The glory goes to rocks that shimmer,
white sidewalks, a rabbit's whiskers, the facets of a crushed
  Pepsi can.
But it might be vain, calling attention to rays
shooting everywhere, touching all it sees
with wit and fluency,

and not a little attitude.
It's washed windows, backlit with the artists' blue
of holy robes, and a touch
of last night's moon.
Brilliant sunshine is not lazy or negligent,

but don't expect leniency. Tremble
for the too ambitious on a *brilliant sunshine* day like this.
They will be stared down
and beaten back
into the pergola's buttercup chair.

MARILYN BUSHMAN-CARLTON

And Where Were You?

—the beginning of the Covid pandemic

Sometimes I worry I will have forgotten
the feel of torsos, arms,
the metronomes of human hearts,
being at Stella's with a friend,
leaning into the spittle of talk
over din of dishes and diners,
innocently opening our mouths,
bumping into strangers at their tasks,
and chatting with dressed-up people
during intermissions or before a movie starts.
Where were you, people ask, when Kennedy died?
Where were you when you first saw the planes
piercing the first, and then the second Tower?
I was not in Paris, Sydney, or Buenos Aires,
but in Palm Springs, not that far away,
staying in a two-bedroom
with my husband and a couple of friends,
spring's blooms set to disappear sooner than we knew.
There we were, going out as we pleased,
pulling the handles of self-serve,
zigzagging through outlets, bargain hunting
just because we could, buying clothes
we didn't know we'd have no place to wear.

Cinnamon in a Pandemic

I hope the cinnamon gone from the store shelves
is blessing those who have it,

that its ancient exotic balm
makes pungent explosions
in cookies, cakes, rice,

dusts arms and noses,
kicks powdery comfort into batters. I hope

its earthy reds toss, partner,
and tumble
into the turbulence of bubbling puddings,
meat pies, oatmeal,

onto buttered toast, waffles,
applesauce, that its contagious well-being

cobbles with blueberries and peaches,
lifts chicken and lamb,

that it twirls and flies, seeps
into cracks of whorled rolls,

hums, spills,
feverishly pours over ice cream,
popcorn, and buttered nuts,

pushing through the insight
and the nonsense of the news.

I hear its satin, time-worn voice,
come, worried ones
in each dash of warmed milk, cocoa, tea.

Open the windows, let it wander
the gray, too-quiet neighborhoods,

let it sift its glory, its puffs of goodness over us,
let it sustain us all.

Winter Meet-ups with Carole
during the Covid Pandemic

"From the seed of a pattern, everything grows."
—Barbara Kingsolver

My sister and I meet in the city cemetery,
collapsible chairs near a sheltering wall distanced apart.
Shrouds of breath whiten the bracing air.

An unlikely place to chat, the air alive
with bacteria, skeletons, dust. Our parents are here,
ancestors, townspeople from our childhoods

though we have not come to practice necromancy.
We know that bones don't speak. We like the solace
of familiar people attending us. Is that Shirley Tripp

tsk-tsking in the leaves? Jo Webb's taciturn applause
echoing through this microcosm of the town that made us
cataloged in tidy streets and intersections,

the town sprawled into then unending fields?
Headstones list births and deaths,
offspring, sometimes legends of wings, lilies,

an occasional photo or poem, often a temple.
We reap the benefaction of the passed-on
who did their best; died satisfied. And praise the miscreants,

the tendentious few whose manicured haunts
belie their dirty-handkerchief lives. Liberated from masks,
we gulp the sharp air shifting through skeletons

of aged trees, hear our mother's raspy dying voice.
Some few arthritic leaves teach how to cling. I want more
   of this,
sitting with my sister, her lips curved and rosy, alive.

Polio

In 1952, the worst polio outbreak in American history
infected 58,000 people, killing more than 3,000, and
paralyzing 21,000, the majority of them children.

—*Time Magazine*, March 29, 1954

Old people are dying of *COVID-19*,
hard of hearing, *Ok Boomers*,

marathon running, cobalt-chromium knee and hip
arthritic *codgers* with slept-in hair,

salon-kempt *biddies*, bald *seniors* with motor homes,
coach class travelers, vinyl record listening,

lowriding, wounded *old coots*, *Vietnam veterans*,
placard-holding bell-bottomed *hippies*,

cigarette smoking, teetotaling *oldsters*,
farmers, artists, nurses, waiters, college educated or not,

with dozens of grandchildren or none, long or thrice married,
single, gay, the *elderly* long ago relieved,

if lucky, of the daily rituals of cooking from scratch,
long days away, carpools and PTA,

the *old* who edited their children's high school essays,
but stared dumbfounded at their first-graders' math,

old duffers, *old farts*, the Medicare-privileged,
senior-discount elderly getting by

with computers, smart phones, HOV lanes, and rushed food,
old timers born in tidy or not-so-tidy childhood

MARILYN BUSHMAN-CARLTON

neighborhoods viciously attacked by polio,
children seen but not heard, children whose summers
   disappeared

to naps, fears of irrigation ditches, swimming pools,
World War II children hunkering under desks, in dark halls,

black and white nightmares of bombs, children
who lay in their beds (and sometimes died) with Asian flu;

the *antiques* of Doris Day, the Beatles, big hair,
Ruby Bridges, women's lib, Kent State, Kennedy

and now this particular enemy virus
hell-bent to get them—

the sacrificial lambs who in 1954
for the largest experiment in modern history

were sent by desperate parents
to the front lines of the war on polio,

an army almost 2 million strong
lining up in schools across America,

and lifting their cotton sleeves
for the Salk polio-vaccine trials,

a vaccine harvested from the kidneys
of live monkeys, made "safer" with a solution

of water-soaked formaldehyde, rock and roll children
now sight impaired, slow drivers,

hard-headed, long-in-the-tooth *old timers*, children
whose innocence did not outweigh

their parents' terror of the highly contagious,
often crippling, permanently withering

or paralyzing horrors of leg braces, wheelchairs,
yellow iron lungs, death itself.

Marriage in Stacked Couplets

—the two of us attempt to glue our
address numbers on a front yard boulder

I want them level, he wants them staggered
    We've a unique pattern of haggling

        We can finish this task while the sun hovers
           It's just four simple numbers!

To complete a task is an ongoing battle
    The picayune details, uneasy laughter

        One of us dallies, can't seem to hurry
           Maddening the other who works in a frenzy

Thank goodness, he can still bedazzle
    With a fetching flex of a working muscle

        After much coaxing and pithy mutinies
           One of us gives, slathers on glue

There's heat in these torches we carry
    Though we're often de trop and weary

        When we lie in tamed silence together
           Neither is fooled by the calm of a breather

Mid-November Rain

Drenched and weary, the cherry tree
I watch from my window holds

doggedly on its thin trunk as the mid-
November storm saturates its roots—

sufficient water to wallow in,
but too little to create a liquid grave.

I take comfort from the hard insistent rain,
its sensibility in sync with my temporary grief,

take comfort in the way the clouds' bulging
coffers let loose to cosset my soul.

Atypically burdened and out of sorts, I
submit the whole of myself to its bruising punch

and moan *O woe is me* to this cold and slumpy day,
to the cherry boughs that keep on

like waitresses paid by the hour,
their feet caught in the cold mud of misery.

MARILYN BUSHMAN-CARLTON

Murmuration

A dap pli n g,
        a dimming, an all-at-once rumble
of hundreds of good for nothing
starlings. An avalanche of ink in the icy
slate-blue, they thicken to pitch, an im-
promptu tumble. Gather and fold,
fleetingly pose: midnight at center,
lyrical ridges, dizzying script.

At once, a whale thrust from the sea,
a geyser, a swan, a sight for sore eyes,
and then some . . .   Acrobatics black-dust in g
hither & thither a fresh slip of snow
on the cold Christmas earth. Thousands
of wings flinging good news. Starlings
unbundle, margins dissolve, wings lengthen

and g l i d e, sling daringly low.
All hail and hallelujah I say to no one
& divine what I can from these ordinarily
misbehaving birds, praise their bonanza
of magnetic plainsong, their lavish
    out bu rst in   g s
                    of grace.

The Basic Tune of the Sparrow

Outside the glass that keeps us warm,
the sparrows,
most common of creatures,
of whom the promise is made
that none will be lost,
are content,
releasing out from themselves
the basic, expected
tune of Sparrow.
They intone through the snows
that flesh the limbs
and starch white the ground
where in rust and green seasons
they forage for food,
take in stride the wider design
be it snow or rain, shards of sun,
the discontent of wind.
They expect nothing more,
accept even less.
Brown feather, small bone, unsung
as late love, bare light bulbs,
a white cotton slip,
they yield.
No murmur   no envy   no pain
leaks from their beaks.

MARILYN BUSHMAN-CARLTON

I Settle into My Other Years

The sediment settles
at my middle,

but it's a satisfactory
memoir,

a decent box
of keepsakes.

The giftbag of my skin
still suffices,

holding the same body
I came with:

slight,
short of stature,

though compacted,
and more precise.

Though I'm nakedly
off-balance,

I'm unabatedly wise.
With each reduction,

the best of me
melds in the sauce.

The Solace of Letting Go

—ending with a line by Mary Oliver

I'll never go back to Brazil, enter another
body of water, take amusement park rides that drop.

No more enduring time on a beach,
deafening concerts, farcical plays.

I'm eschewing tall shoes, unstable stools,
skinny jeans, being told what to eat.

Karaoke, new gadgets, slippery surfaces, cheddar cheese.
Suppressing (most) advice to my children.

Bye-bye fickle friends, tedious meetings,
over-apologizing, toeing the line. Letting go of all

but certain regrets, an ounce of foolishness,
and the right to begin something new.

I'm digging out, making room for extravagant abundance
of nothing at all, for the sharper relief of absence.

Think winter tree after the lift of a council of crows.
Give me what's empty—ladles, palms facing up,

the well of a magician's black hat.
Hand me baskets, buckets, the biggest blue bowls,

anything spilled of what-ifs, lies, what you'd expect.
Let me cherish the lone patch of dirt wanting rain,

Monday morning chapels. Give me a sky *washed blue*
and emptied entirely of [what's] second-rate.

Procedure

Because of my allergic reaction
to anesthesia,
I choose to be awake

for the short procedure.
I'm gurney-delivered
to the industrial,

meat-locker-cold surgical room
where my body shifts
to a slab

slim as a pauper's coffin,
and young hands proceed
to bury me

in blue steri-cloths,
layering them
over my body, and finally my face,
leaving open only
a squarish bullseye
around my heart where a

superficially interred
monitoring device
will be exhumed.

Fingers, lots of them,
swipe yards of tape into place
and tamp it down.

When I try to lift my arms,
I find I'm bound,
and claustrophobia

kicks in. I inhale deeply
the lifeline of oxygen
taped to my philtrum,

and through the filmy
face covering,
fix my eyes on diluted blue,

and then intense light
recalled by some
who temporarily

cast off their earthly bodies,
but made it back to tell.

The Dermatologist

"How ya doin', Kiddo?" he asks
as he bounds into the room,
his white coat flying.
I see him annually now,
this time in a different office,
spanking new, unlike either of us.
Close at hand is his canister
of liquid nitrogen,
the ice that burns,
an oxymoron like his "Kiddo"
and the fact that he rides a stool
with wheels. He grins
like a boy from our hazy childhoods,
and then he's down to business,
his hands and eyes scanning
my tarnished epidermis,
even the bottoms of my feet,
using erudite terms like *acanthosis,*
papules, seborrheic keratosis,
then chooses which two
old-age pop-ups to banish
with his 320-degree-below-zero bonfire.

At the Nail Salon

Is it time to let the nails go, I wonder.
Why draw attention with polish,
especially Spring shades
like lavender, a color my grandmother wore?

Why display the burdens
these hands have borne?
Why lay bare my life, its length and habits,
its mercies and sorrows,

its tempests and extremities?
Aware of the young technician's touch,
I look into her smile,
her lifted face, her attentive eyes.

My nails are finished, but she is not.
She embraces
each used hand, and kneads,
daubing miracles
to irrigate the lines. The deep,

drawn vertical caresses
humble my disgrace,
soothe like a lullaby. Her breath is sweet,
alive, intimate. She is not frightened by the ruins

of my long journey,
nor of the tithes a body must make.

MARILYN BUSHMAN-CARLTON

Lingering

Even after long visits, the children linger.
They linger after they say they'd better go;

when they stand; take the first steps.
Their father and I saunter with them to their cars

where we linger together in the dust of nascent stars,
in the twilight the French call *l'heure*.

Clouds meander over the cola-colored sky
like scattered picnic cloths

patching the blacktop driveway where we linger
as the moon rises and night

nudges the backs of our necks.
We sense a frisson afoot, and stay put, reboot,

seize a cooling second wind.
I love the way each new hour unmasks

the daylight faces of those I love,
how pupils deepen with melancholy topics,

constrict with the weight of the grave. How
night uncurtains public guises,

loosens the loops and lines of language.
I love the drowsy burbling, the out-of-control giggling,

the garbled phrases, the copacetic tears.
How one memory recalls another as we stay

corded to the moon, it's lesser light
warping tomorrow's ho-hum world.

We're a bunch, toes exposed in flip flops,
hair wilted, stomach muscles sloppy.

We're perfect laggards
languishing to satiation in the late summer air.

MARILYN BUSHMAN-CARLTON

The Granddaughters Wear My Clothes

At season's end, I offer those that no longer flatter
my body of balsa bone and wan, diaphanous skin
to my teenage granddaughters.

They try them on in my bedroom leaving
unapologetically what they don't want
folded on my bed and closet floor. I'll recognize

my leopard print blouse with the tails knotted
above a bare torso, my jeans newly-ripped and shimmied low,
a dressy skirt paired charmingly with leather ankle boots.

I'll learn how I might have poked a width of pistachio shirt
into baggy ink-blue jeans. What pleasure to see
my carefully-chosen garments articulated by bodies

of climbers, dancers, swimmers, to see collars magnify
moist basins at the swallows of nubile throats.
I've no self-pity for this aging body that's had its run,

think more about concealing than decorating it.
It's their turn now for clothes to hug florescent bodies,
their turn to swing lissome arms and legs (a marinade of tones)

from brief sleeves, skirts, and shorts, their turn
to trip into the summer grass of their enormous lives,
unsuspicious of their beauty.

O Morning Glory

I hate you. I do. You often break my heart.
Were you in Eden, or a volunteer

for the cold and dreary now? No matter,
your blooms beguile me, your demitasse faces,

your little laps balancing drops of dew.
I love your looping vines, your leaves—

rowboats racing for the shore.
But how can I trust you, the way you hurry

like cancer. Or gossip. Or grow malicious
like vain girls blossoming

with cocksure loveliness.
O morning glory, seeker of wider skies,

I understand your need to stretch and climb,
to dash while those around you trundle.

What's not to love of your headstrong recklessness,
your blunt call to bee and butterfly,

the lissome garden snake, by a woman frantic
to kill you off, a woman who simply has to pause

and smell your white, ambrosial breath,
finger each rogue blossom.

Statistics Say You'll Die First

—fifteen reflections

1.

Our friends are dying. Angels pump their wings over our
    storybook lives.
So blessed that asking more seems obscene, but I'm asking.

2.

I thought we'd feel old. But our bodies, like seasons, are
    confused.
Our friends are dying. What will I do? How will I live?

3.

Those sepia snapshots our parents saw in their old-time
    cameras
will be my shade of everything, of everywhere I go.

4.

Days and hours sprint past us now. The grace and foibles fly.
    I'll sell
the big car, cushion your absence with daisies, thunder the
    house with music.

5.

I've seen that torpid look in a deserted spouse's eyes: suddenly
    gray,
hollow; not just old, but elderly now, yellow pin-pricks of fear.

6.

Vacancy so vast it reverberates, worships with the
    abandoned in the small spaces
where they hold themselves, nursing the unlaced interlace
    of the one who's gone.

7.
Familiar syncopated syllables will undo me: a brief olfactory
   illumination,
a quizzical or skeptical look, the begging question of how
   to live.

8.
Let me bottle up that whistling, love, I'd hardly heard
until that day I did, sweet and intimate as sleep-tossed sheets.

9.
With whom will I banter, whose needling dodge, whose
   tongue-flipping
repostes, reposte? From whom hear *what* from the next room?

10.
Who will assume the kitchen castle; wide-armed, peel the
   carrots
while I zig and zag to measure spices, stir the soup?

11.
I'll feel your draft at my side, your breath over my shoulder,
   your elan
smoking under my feet, your absence in the off-kilter bed.

12.
How to stay the disconnecting dots, do without the missing
   yang,
the catch phrase, the rest of the laugh, the other half of most
   of my life?

13.
When you disappear into the trees and sky, who will travel
 with me,
be the first reader of my poems, love the children as I do,
 be my daily first and last?

14.
I'll forage though your things like a stalker, frantic for any
 vestigial hints of you,
for bulletins in the scattered post-its, for any facsimile of
 our melded lives.

15.
How not smell you in the snow's whiteness, in the
 denouement of fall's falling rain?
How not miss the sentiment of your hands waking up my
 skin?

Home Again

I wait at the airport curb, a suitcase of laundry beside me.
I'd expected cold, but you never know in Utah
in late October. A thin breeze fingers my frizzled hair,
letting fibers fly, and penetrates each pore
as it seeps into my homesick lungs.
A white moon dominates, and I do what it asks:
tilt up, open wide, and lean into it, glad as a child.
I'll take it, and tomorrow, too, standing at my window
watching wind sling weathered leaves,
savoring the cupboard smells of expiration, breathing
the barely-just lavender scrub oak bunched between
what might well be a chorus of redheads on the hill.

Acknowledgements

The following poems first appeared in the publications indicated: "We Wore Dresses" in *Quartet Magazine*; "Desire" and "The Proposal," in *Sunstone*; "Hair Narratives" in *Psaltery and Lyre*; "Irresistible Burdens" and "Learning to Touch," in *BYU Studies*; "Sunday School," "Judas," and "A Found Poem" in *Dialogue: A Journal of Mormon Thought*; "One Missing," "Just a Boy," "Thin," "My Maiden Name" and "The Granddaughters Wear My Clothes" in *Segullah*.

"My Mother (who is in Heaven) Meets Heavenly Mother," appears in the anthology, *Dove Song: Heavenly Mother in Mormon Poetry*. "Cinnamon in a Pandemic" and "And Where Were You" appear in *The Art of Isolation: an Anthology of Poetry and Art*; "Who Needs You Anyway" and "At the Nail Salon" appear in *SLCC Community Anthology*.

"The Basic Tune of the Sparrow" was first published in *Cheat Grass*, by the Utah State Poetry Society. "Our Spot in Millcreek Canyon," "Forget-Me-Nots," and "Barbed Wire and Cardinals" first appeared in *Pulchritudinous and Other Ways to Say Beautiful*, by Lulu Press.

Thanks to the Lehi Free Press for featuring many of these poems in the pages of itsnewspaper.

The author wishes to thank writing partner Holly Welker, who along with Darlene Young and Susan Howe, read and offered suggestions on many of these poems and, who along with Lisa Bickmore, blurbed the book; husband, Blaine Carlton for his legal eye and love, and her children and grandchildren for their love and inspiration for many of these poems. Thanks to Joyce Ellen Davis (1939–2022), a wonderful, but unsung, poet, for writing poems I read again and again, and for offering quiet encouragement and support.

MARILYN BUSHMAN-CARLTON

Marilyn Bushman-Carlton has published three books of poetry: *on keeping things small*, (Signature Books 1995); *Cheat Grass*, (1999), which won the Pearle M. Olsen Book Publication/USPS Poet of the Year award, and *Her Side of It* (Signature Books, 2010), winner of the Association of Mormon Letters Poetry award (2010). A chapbook version of *Her Side of It* was a finalist in Comstock Review's 2005 Jess Bryce Niles Chapbook competition. She has also authored a book of children's poems, *Pulchritudinous and Other Ways to Say Beautiful*, for her sixteen grandchildren (Lulu Press, 2015).

Her prose includes a biography, *Worthy: A Young Woman from a Background of Poverty and Abuse Falls Prey to a Polygamous Cult*, (Lulu Press, 2016), a finalist for the 11th Annual Indie Excellence Award. An essay, "The World We Share," appeared in *Baring Witness: 36 Mormon Woman Talk Candidly about, Love, Sex, and Marriage.*

Other awards include a prize (1997) and a grant (1996) from the Utah Arts Council for whom she was an Artist-in-Residence, traveling throughout Utah to teach poetry in elementary, middle, and senior high schools (1996–2012); and awards for individual poems in the *Comstock Review*, the *Ledge*, *The Sow's Ear*, *BYU Studies*, Utah State and National Poetry Societies, Red Butte Gardens, UTA Poetry on the Bus, and others.

Individual poems appear in *Dove Song: Heavenly Mother in Mormon Poetry*; *Fire in the Pasture: Twenty-first Century Mormon Poets*; *Discoveries: Two Centuries of Poems by Mormon Women*; *SLCC Anthology* (2018 and 2020); *Utah Sings* (Vols. 7, 8, & 9); *To Rejoice as Women: Talks from the 1994 Women's Conference*; and other anthologies. Her poems have been featured in *Earth's Daughters*, *Iris*, *Ellipsis*, the *Comstock Review*, among others.

"We Wore Dresses" was nominated for a Pushcart Prize by *Quartet Magazine* (2022).

Marilyn is the mother of five children and sixteen grandchildren and lives in the mountains above Draper, Utah with her husband, Blaine.